Living in Harmony with the Real World

Perfecting our Inner Parenting

Card Set

Gary Edward Gedall

Published by

From Words to Worlds

Lausanne, Switzerland

www.fromwordstoworlds.com

ISBN : 978-2-940535-76-7

Dear Reader,

I would presume that you either have bought the main book or are quite clear as to the concept and how to use the cards.

So, I will limit my introduction to just reminding you that your first task is to find the images that best describe your main inner parents or coping strategies, at this time.

Then reflect on the situations that you find yourself in where they don't work very well.

Then, look through the other cards and descriptions, to see what other ways of dealing with yourself and outside situations might work better for you.

From there, it is a process of thinking about meditating on and practising the attitudes and skills of your new parent archetype.

I wish you both fun and success.

Please feel free to write to me if you have any comments or feedback, and of course, any reviews or sharing about this book would be greatly appreciated.

With my kindest regards,

Gary Edward Gedall,

Lausanne, Switzerland 14 08 2022
gary.gedall@bluewin.ch

The Nudist

The Belayer

Knight in Armour

The Builder

The Belayer

The Belayer is the person who ensures the security of those that take risks.

Taking risks is essential to having a full, interesting and exciting life.

However, disaster will find you if you refuse to take the proper precautions!

Being too careful can also be a problem.

Sometimes life offers us opportunities that include risks for which we have neither the time nor the means to guarantee our security.

The Nudist

The Nudist represents a state of total vulnerability.

In most conflict situations, the usual reaction is eithe to leave, to defend oneself or (counter) attack the other.

The nudist does none of these, they accept all feedback as interesting and potentially helpful information.

Taking on all criticisms without the distance or ability to assess whether the person giving the information is a person of confidence or not can lead to accepting inappropriate feedback.

The Builder

The Builder takes a plan and creates an actual project from it.

The Builder is a doer; they take an idea, a dream and materialise it.

The Builder knows that success comes from consistent effort.

Taking someone else's plan, without using your own competence and experience to assess whether it makes sense to you, can lead you to disaster.

Always keep the possibility to use your own judgement.

Knight in Armour

The Knight in Armour is someone that is well protected from the pain and suffering coming from people or outside events.

Being either too sensitive in general or forced to encounter difficult situations or persons can be particularly difficult to cope with.

Learning to protect and passively defend oneself will make life much more copeable.

Cutting oneself emotionally from others can leave us cold, friendless and lacking support when we, ourselves might be in need of an empathic carer.

The Champion

The Fan

The Diplomat

The Sergeant Major

The Fan

The Fan knows just how fabulous we are.

No matter what is happening in our lives, subjective, professional, intimate or whatever, the Fan will always see us in a positive light.

Whenever you might start to lose confidence in yourself and your future, call on your Fan.

Knowing, somewhere, that you are great is a boost that we all can need

We could be in danger of over-inflating our egos.

The Champion

It is fitting, proper, educational and valorising to fight and win our own battles.

However, we do not always have the means to deal with certain situations ourselves, physical, mental, emotional, experiential or otherwise.

When it is essential to seek out, and accept the help of someone more capable of doing this for us.

If we become over-habituated to having others fight our battles for us, we will lose the ability to defend ourselves.

The Sergeant Major

The Sergeant Major is the epitome of 'tough love'.

When we can't be bothered, feel too tired, are ready to give up.

Then we need to call for the Sergeant Major.

Effort, tenacity, focus and hard work will bring you the results you dream of.

We need to always stay aware of the limits of our comfort zones.

The Diplomat

The Diplomat knows how to give without losing.
Most of us live in a polarity of winning or losing.
Most of us base our self-image on being right and proving the other wrong.
Most of us lose, even if, in the moment, we win.
Learn to win through compromise.

The expectation and desire to find a win-win solution is not always possible.

The Coach

The Critic

The Policeman

The Accountant

The Critic

The Critic has the knowledge, culture and appreciation to be able to assess the value of the production that they are presented with.

A critic's reflection might be positive or negative but always based on a sound understanding of the piece and full of useful advice.

Negative Aspects

A critic is only a person, if you are not totally convinced by the assessment of one critic, nothing stops you from getting a second opinion.

The Coach

The Coach is positive, pushy and presses for perfection.

However, they are also sensitive, supportive and centred on the success of the person being coached.

In the end, it is the person themselves, who alone, will have to face and compete against the opposition.

Negative Aspects

We can become too dependent on having someone to support and motivate us.

The Accountant

The Accountant works with the facts.

They quietly and coolly add up the figures and inform us of their calculations.

Keeping an emotional distance from a 'hot' situation allows one the space to assess and analyse it.

One sees clearly through calm waters.

Negative Aspects

There is always the danger of ignoring one's own feelings and the feelings of others.

The Policeman

The Policeman is there to inform on and uphold the rules.

They neither make them nor judge whether someone is guilty of something or not.

Their function is not to punish.

Choose to ignore them at your peril.

Negative Aspects

The policeman has no part in the creation of the rules.

The Teacher

The Rebel

The Walker

The Judge

The Judge is an impartial assessor.

Their task is to investigate the facts and to conclude the appropriateness of an act or action in relation to the relevant laws or rules in vigour.

Justice might be blind, but it need not be heartless.

Negative Aspects

If we find ourselves too often in the mode of the judge, we are in danger of missing out on life's experiences and might well find ourselves acting superior to those around us.

The Teacher

The Teacher sees life as a series of lessons to learn and an endless opportunity to grow and develop.

The more intensely, positive or negative, an event is experienced, then the greater the possibility there is to benefit from it.

Learn from life, and you can only grow.

Negative Aspects

Treating all life events as lessons can lead one to become too passive and less proactive.

The Walker

The Walker is in for the long haul.

The Chinese proverb states that; "A journey of a thousand miles begins with a single step".

What it fails to mention is that it must be followed by another, and another.

"Slow and steady wins the race".

Negative Aspects

"Slow and steady wins the race". Sometimes, slow and steady, might well offer too much opportunity for one's competitors to succeed in your place.

The Rebel

The Rebel knows the official rules but does not accept them.

However, the Rebel is neither an anarchist nor a nihilist.
They have their own sets of values and morals which they acknowledge and follow.

Being a Rebel means opposing the establishment in favour of a more just and moral order.

Negative Aspects

Choosing to not follow the rules brings with it a huge responsibility.

The Salesman

The Juggler

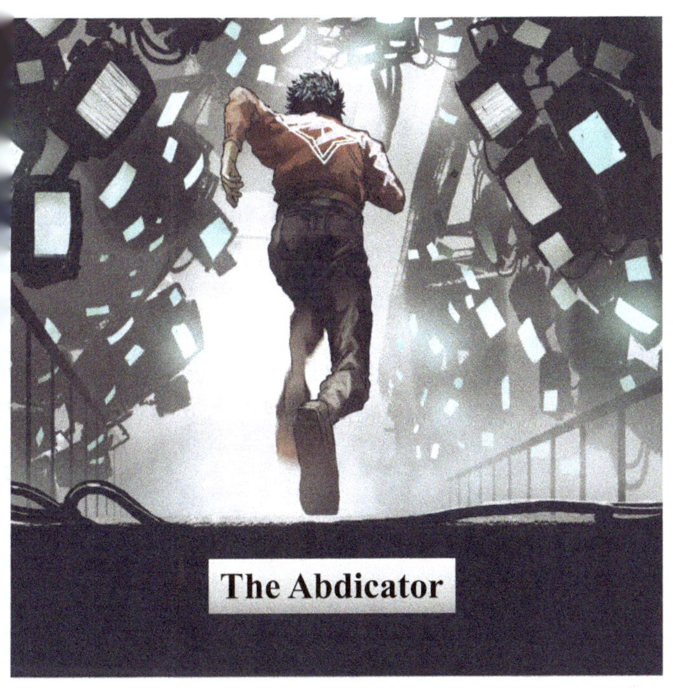

The Abdicator

The Chess Master

The Juggler

he Juggler can deal with many things at the same time.

Being able to juggle many balls at once, for many of us, can be a most difficult challenge.

However, while keeping a vague awareness of all that you are doing, only focus on the one specific task that you are involved in at the moment.

Negative Aspects

Trying to keep too many 'balls in the air', at any one time can end very, very badly and we can find ourselves dropping all of them.

The Salesman

The Salesman is not known for being the most honest or trustworthy of types.

Although, pointing out the best aspects of someone or something can be a useful skill to possess.

Being completely and strictly honest are admirable qualities in general. However, there are circumstances when life is not always so correct ...

Negative Aspects

Don't allow yourself to be taken over by the 'dark side' of comfort lying.

The Chess Master

The Chess Master is the strategist.

Stop, look, think, understand and plan before you move.

Acting quickly, without reflection can lead you into worse and worse situations.

Negative Aspects

One can totally over think a situation, and while we are looking five or ten moves ahead, our opponent has found a small error that we have failed to notice and has succeeded against us.

The Abdicator

The Abdicator is he who gives up.

Giving up is not an action that is highly regarded in our modern society. However, being able to release our investments; can, at times, be necessary.

"He who fights and runs away, … lives to fight another day."

Negative Aspects

Getting into the habit of giving up too easily is the perfect recipe for never finishing or succeeding in anything.

The Runner

The Watchmaker

The Gun Slinger

The Sumo

The Watchmaker

The Watchmaker is a perfectionist.

There is only one way to make a watch that works - exactly. There are times when only going that extra mile to make it right, will do.

"Do it right the first time, and it will be the only time."

'Perfection can be the royal route to failure', a concept that I often reflect on with my anxious patients.

The Runner

The Runner advances, and at speed.

There are times when we need to take all our energy, desire and effort and run with it.

Now is the time to show the world that you are someone to be taken seriously.

Go for it!

Running through life can take us a really long way, However, it is often the journey that brings quality and value, not just arriving.

The Sumo

The Sumo stands his ground.

He is solid, sure and static until he chooses to move.

Being able to resist, to absorb the various attacks of others, can be very useful and advantageous. Too often in life, reacting can be seen and felt as a sign of weakness.

Stand your ground, and wait your moment.

Heaviness, slowness and inertia can be very negative traits.

The Gun Slinger

The Gun Slinger lives or dies in a heartbeat. Immediate reactivity is the ultimate survival necessity.

However, a keen awareness of all that is happening or is likely to happen, at any moment, is also part of this package.

Be aware, be ready to react, react.

Operating at a life-or-death speed can certainly save your life, but might also, accidentally take the life of another.

The Dancer

The Expressionist

Daddy Cool

Daddy Cool is cool.

Sometimes it just feels right to lie back and let the world rush by.

Now is the time to de-stress, relax, and recharge your batteries.

Today is officially, an unofficial holiday.

Negative Aspects

Taking it easy is a most important, however, if it becomes a lifestyle, you may find quite quickly that it is going nowhere.

The Dancer

The Dancer understands the rhythms and flows of life.

They turn, they sway, they dip and dive. And yet their personal space is never impeached upon.

A dancer knows how to manoeuvre through life; gently, elegantly, yet free from the restrictions imposed by others.

Negative Aspects

Elegantly avoiding any clash or conflict can be a very comfortable way to manoeuvre through life. Yet, sometimes we need to protect some territory and accept to bump heads.

The Clown

The Clown pokes fun at the awful seriousness of our cold, hard, spiteful, unfair reality.

What this does change, is our appreciation and emotional experience of both internal and external events.

Cry tears of sadness or tears of laughter, the choice is yours.

Negative Aspects

Sometimes, things do have to be taken seriously. Laughter can become a way of avoiding difficult situations and decisions.

The Expressionist

The Expressionist has no interest in limiting themselves to fine details.

It is the broad strokes; brainstorming pipe dreaming, run-it-up-the-flagpole creative moment.

It is the 'let's get something done and see how it looks', moment.

Negative Aspects

There are times when spontaneous creativity and immediate, free expression might be appropriate.

The Rider

The Sailor

The Balloonist

The Farmer

The Sailor

The Sailor navigates the seas and oceans of life.

Our lives can be clear, calm and comfortable.

At other times, the rivers are rough, the seas stormy, and the wind whips the waves into walls of fury.

Ride the storm and keep on course.

Negative Aspects
Sometimes, we really can neither overcome nor avoid a difficult moment.

The Rider

The Rider is a human astride a horse.

The horse is bigger, heavier and much, much more powerful.

An experienced Rider will know how to allow the horse to express its needs, all the while succeeding to keep a firm hold of the reins, keeping them both safe and on the right path.

Negative Aspects
There is a very delicate balance between giving people 'free-rein' in a situation, and keeping a tight rein and blocking all movement and creativity.

The Farmer

The Farmer understands about the seasons.

The Farmer understands about time.

The Farmer prepares his land; plants his seeds, feeds and waters them, and waits.

The Farmer understands patience.

Negative Aspects
Patience is a virtue, virtue is a grace
If you move too slowly, you'll likely lose the race.

The Balloonist

The Balloonist rises above.

There might be wars, revolts, strikes or uprisings.

There are times in our lives when rising above a situation; to get a higher, fuller, dispassionate view, can give us the perspective that we need,

Negative Aspects
Taking distance as a perfect way to avoid difficult situations, maybe too perfect.

Being above, superior, or detached can also be a

The Laser Operator

The Captain

The Linesman

The Surfer

The Captain

The Captain cares for the overall well-being of his crew and the success of his mission.

The Captain goes down with his ship, and will, if necessary, sacrifice himself for the safety of his people.

Take command, take responsibility, and take pride in your task.

Negative Aspects

The Captain, although in command of their ship and responsible for it is still capable and open to listening to the advice of their crew.

The Laser Operator

The Laser Operator understands focus.

There are projects and moments in our lives when everything that distracts us from the important job in hand needs to be put aside.

Small focus, big light.

Negative Aspects

Obviously, by focussing on a very limited portion of your life, you definitely risk the possibility of missing something on major importance.

The Surfer

The Surfer rides the waves.

If one tries to block or resist a powerful force, then that force will crush you.

If you take that force and use it to carry you forward, then it will be your greatest ally.

Negative Aspects

Riding the waves gives us the freedom to be aware of the direction that life is pushing us towards, without allowing it to hamper our independence.

This can be a wonderful thing, or not.

The Linesman

The Linesman is responsible to keep us 'in line'.

Without clear limits, we can easily find ourselves, 'all over the place'.

A helping hand and watchful eye to stop us from straying out from our chosen and necessary path is a support, not a limitation.

Negative Aspects

Staying always within the confines of society's rules, or your group's norms can become very restrictive and hamper your ability to express yourself as a complete and rich human being.

The Seducer

The Ornithologist

The Big Boss

The Gambler

The Ornithologist

The Ornithologist, or Bird Watcher, creates a camouflaged hut, a hide and waits to discover and record what is seen.

They are so discrete, that they are invisible.

To know and understand what is truly happening is of real value.

Negative Aspects

Hiding in plain site is a very interesting strategy.

However, being an invisible person might be both a protection but also an enormous handicap.

The Seducer

The seducer offers dreams in exchange for benefits.

They neither force nor steal. They offer the person feelings of pleasure or satisfaction.

Soft, subtle and sweetly seductive

Negative Aspects

Finding ways to get what you wish for in life can be most pleasant.

However, not learning how to, and the pleasure of, working to earn something through your own direct efforts can leave you emotionally weak and helpless.

The Gambler

The Gambler takes risks.

The good gambler takes risks based on their ability to judge.

A good gambler knows how to judge when a risk is worth gambling on.

A good gambler wins much more than they lose.

Negative Aspects

Sometimes we are so convinced that something is right that we are willing to gamble everything on it.

Sometimes we can be wrong!

The Big Boss

The Big Boss is someone who takes on total control and total responsibility when things get tough.

They trust themselves to cope with difficult situations more than anyone else.

When the going gets tough,

The boss gets going.

Negative Aspects

Taking all the important decisions, can be most destructive in many relationships situations.

The
Rollercoaster
Guy

The Risk Assessor

The Do-It-Yourselfer

Atlas

The Risk Assessor

Life is a risky business.

If we take unreasonable risks, we are likely to suffer major losses.

If we stay unreasonably safe, we will suffer major boredom. If we fear too much for the future, we will wreck the present.

Negative Aspects

If every twist and turn of your life demands a deep risk assessment, life will pass you by before you finish your calculations.

Rollercoaster Guy

Life has its ups and downs, take each moment for what it is, good or bad, it won't last.

Sometimes we have no control over what is happening to us – so just release and go where life takes us.

Living in the moment is very important, but time is a stream, go with the flow.

Negative Aspects

Feeling that we have no control over our lives can lead to feelings of helplessness and depression.

Letting go needs to be carefully dosed.

Atlas

Carries the world on his shoulders

They accept the responsibility for all others

They will accept this heavy burden until they can find someone else to take it on.

Negative Aspects

The ego boost of being the Titan, the Superman, (or Woman), can be enormous.

However, do not let your ego trick you into taking on tasks that are much too heavy and which is impossible to release.

The Do-It-Yourselfer

The Do-It-Yourselfer likes to get things done.

There are times and places where and when quality and precision are necessary or desirable.

There are times and places where and when time and resources are worth investing to achieve a high-value result.

There are also times when 'getting the job done', is the thing to do.

Negative Aspects

Nobody should plan to do a 'shoddy' job of work.

The Pacemaker

The Warrior

The Sannyasin Beggar

The Judo Master

The Warrior

The Warrior is brave, proud and courageous.

Sometimes we need to risk our physical, financial, social, professional and relationship lives.

Sometimes we need to trust that 'Death or Glory' can be right choice.

Heading head-first into a clearly dangerous situation must not be taken lightly.

The damage to yourself or others can be considerable.

The Pacemaker

The Pacemaker has an interesting function in life.

Their strength and utility is leading through example.   In fact, it can easily seem that they have no interest in you at all, as they often tend to focus on their job in hand.

However, by following their example, they can lead you to success.

Helping and supporting others to succeed is a wonderful and noble undertaking.

However, sometimes we must win our own races.

The Judo Master

(S)he who uses the strength of others against themselves.

When we are pitted against a foe of superior force.

Direct confrontation will only lead to failure.

Do not try to win.

Allow them to lose.

This can only work against an active opponent that is using their power directly against you.

The Sannyasin Beggar

The Sannyasin Beggar owns nothing.

They acquire nothing

They wish for nothing

Nothing is everything for them

Before taking such a stance one must be totally clear that they are ready to renounce all worldly goods, status and power.